HANDY
LITTLE
GUIDE

Fasting

Deacon Greg Kandra

Our Sunday Visitor
Huntington, Indiana

Nihil Obstat
Msgr. Michael Heintz, Ph.D.
Censor Librorum

Imprimatur
✠ Kevin C. Rhoades
Bishop of Fort Wayne-South Bend
February 16, 2024

The *Nihil Obstat* and *Imprimatur* are official declarations that a book is free from doctrinal or moral error. It is not implied that those who have granted the *Nihil Obstat* and *Imprimatur* agree with the contents, opinions, or statements expressed.

Scripture texts in this work are taken from the *New American Bible*, revised edition © 2010, 1991, 1986, 1970 Confraternity of Christian Doctrine, Inc., Washington, D.C. and are used by permission of the copyright owner. All Rights Reserved. No part of the New American Bible may be reproduced in any form without permission in writing from the copyright owner.

Excerpts from the English translation of the *Catechism of the Catholic Church* for use in the United States of America Copyright © 1994, United States Catholic Conference, Inc.—Libreria Editrice Vaticana. Used with Permission. English translation of the *Catechism of the Catholic Church*: Modifications from the Editio Typica copyright © 1997, United States Conference of Catholic Bishops—Libreria Editrice Vaticana.

Every reasonable effort has been made to determine copyright holders of excerpted materials and to secure permissions as needed. If any copyrighted materials have been inadvertently used in this work without proper credit being given in one form or another, please notify Our Sunday Visitor in writing so that future printings of this work may be corrected accordingly.

Our Sunday Visitor Publishing Division, Our Sunday Visitor, Inc., 200 Noll Plaza, Huntington, IN 46750; www.osv.com; 1-800-348-2440

ISBN: 978-1-63966-173-2 (Inventory No. T2874)

1. RELIGION—Christian Living—Prayer.
2. RELIGION—Christian Living—Spiritual Growth.
3. RELIGION—Christianity—Catholic.
eISBN: 978-1-63966-174-9
LCCN: 2024933022

Cover and interior design: Amanda Falk
Cover and interior art: AdobeStock

PRINTED IN THE UNITED STATES OF AMERICA

Contents

INTRODUCTION
What This Book Is and Isn't

If we're honest, most of us struggle to eat well, eat sensibly, and eat healthy. For Catholics, the struggle can take on another dimension when we try to give up eating altogether and undertake one of the most venerable religious traditions in the world: a fast.

Fasting can be mysterious and intimidating, but it doesn't have to be. This little book, I hope, will help make this practice understandable and doable. Fasting isn't just for the extremely pious or for ascetics who subsist on water and air while living in a cave. Anyone can do it.

With that said, let me define what this book is and isn't, and what you can expect from the little guide you hold in your hands.

First, this is not the place to learn about the latest dieting fads, trends, gimmicks, or techniques. I'm not going to recommend different types of intermittent fasting or offer a new health regimen that will enrich your life and change your waist size. I'm not a doctor or a health guru. (Just ask my wife, who rolls her eyes every time I order waffle fries at Chick-fil-A.) In fact, I struggle with fasting. I'm a deacon and a writer who, as I write this, is desperate for some cookie dough ice cream.

Second, this is not a book with recipes or dietary plans. What you will find is one recipe that pervades throughout this whole book — a way to blend the ingredients of faith and fortitude to make fasting spiritually fulfilling.

What I provide in the following pages are ideas, inspiration, insights, and prayers that can help turn the difficult (and don't fool yourself: it *should* be difficult) goal of fasting into an encounter that may leave you hungry but can still leave you feeling fed. The real point of fasting is to take away the incomparable pleasure of eating in order to turn our thoughts and desires elsewhere.

How can we do that? And how can we do it better?

If you're looking for answers to those questions and more, you've come to the right place.

This book offers an approach to see fasting not as a chore or a duty — or a painful discipline that looms over us during Lent — but rather to see this age-old practice as an opportunity to give something up and, in the process, just give.

This sacrifice becomes a gift that keeps giving.

Consider this handy guide as a faith-filled whisper reminding you to refrain when one hand is reaching for that bag of potato chips you saw in the kitchen while the other is gripping the rosary in your pocket and you're trying, very hard, to just say no.

Take a few moments here and now to

just say yes.

Say yes to experiencing fasting in a new way.

Say yes to feeling a few hunger pangs, but also to feeling a small but powerful connection to all the hungry of the world.

Say yes to drawing closer to Christ, who knew what it was to be human and, before embarking on the great mission of his earthly life, spent time in the desert to suffer loneliness and hardship and, above all, hunger.

We all hunger for something. Fasting can help us reconsider our yearnings and appetites, during which we often find that those desires are for more than mere food.

One of the lessons of fasting is coming to the realization that other things are more important than food. (I know, I often have a hard time believing that, too.)

Let's get started. And let's begin with a prayer.

A Prayer Before Beginning a Fast

Almighty God, you created food for nourishment, fulfillment, satisfaction, and pleasure. The blessing of food brings people together, binds us as a community, and enriches our lives. Thank you for this gift! And thank you for the opportunity to surrender this gift in a period of fasting, a period that I pray will bring me closer to my brothers and sisters around the world and ultimately draw me closer to you, the One whose love feeds every hunger. Walk with me on this journey of fasting that I may one day enjoy feasting at your heavenly banquet, beside your Son, who made of himself a feast for all humanity in his gift of the Eucharist. I pray all this with joyful hope and

a heart that hungers to be with you forever.
Amen.

1
A Brief (or Fast) History of Fasting

Before we jump into *how* to fast, we should understand *why* we fast and where the notion of religious or spiritual fasting originated.

First, you will find fasting in many religious traditions, not just Judeo-Christian. The good people at the *Encyclopedia Britannica* offer some examples:

> In the religions of ancient peoples and civilizations, fasting was a practice to prepare persons, especially priests and priestesses, to approach the deities. In the Hellenistic mystery religions, the gods

were thought to reveal their divine teachings in dreams and visions only after a fast that required the total dedication of the devotees. Among the pre-Columbian peoples of Peru, fasting often was one of the requirements for penance after an individual had confessed sins before a priest.

Fasting remains an integral part of many religions to this day. We can trace our Christian practice of fasting back to our Jewish forebearers.

The holiest day of the year for Jews is Yom Kippur, and the Torah explains that fasting is an integral part of that day of prayer and repentance. The Book of Leviticus stipulates that the Day of Atonement should be one of self-denial (see 23:26–30).

According to the website Chabat.org, the history of fasting on Yom Kippur traces its origins to the days when the Jews left Egypt and sinned by worshiping a golden calf in the desert. Fasting is thus a form of atonement. Jewish educator Aliza Bulow writes, "The purpose of fasting is to bring one to repent, and true repentance brings about a change in actions."

With this history as precedent, we progress to the most famous fast in the New Testament, practiced by Jesus Christ for forty days in the desert. We hear about that event every year at the beginning of Lent, and it really sets the stage for our own forty days of prayer, fasting, and almsgiving.

Why did Jesus undertake that fast? And what does his example have to say to each of us who seeks to follow (on a more modest scale) his example?

Here's some wisdom from Pope Benedict, who spoke about Jesus' fasting in one of his messages for the beginning of Lent:

> We might wonder what value and meaning there is for us Christians in depriving ourselves of something that in itself is good and

useful for our bodily sustenance. The Sacred Scriptures and the entire Christian tradition teach that fasting is a great help to avoid sin and all that leads to it.

In the New Testament, Jesus brings to light the profound motive for fasting, condemning the attitude of the Pharisees, who scrupulously observed the prescriptions of the law, but whose hearts were far from God. True fasting, as the divine Master repeats elsewhere, is rather to do the will of the heavenly Father, who "sees in secret, and will reward you" (Mt 6:18). He himself sets the example, answering Satan, at the end of the forty days spent in the desert that "man shall not live by bread alone, but by every word that proceeds from the mouth of God" (Mt 4:4). The true fast is thus directed to eating the "true food," which is to do the

Father's will (cf. Jn 4:34)."

Benedict concludes with an insight that points to why Jesus fasted — and why we should do it as well:

> It seems abundantly clear that fasting represents an important ascetical practice, a spiritual arm to do battle against every possible disordered attachment to ourselves. Freely chosen detachment from the pleasure of food and other material goods helps the disciple of Christ to control the appetites of nature, weakened by original sin, whose negative effects impact the entire human person. ... It is good to see how the ultimate goal of fasting is to help each one of us, as ... Pope John Paul II wrote, to make the complete gift of self to God.

So, what can we take from this?

First, fasting is as old as time. Elements of fasting are apparent in countless traditions and religions, from a variety of cultures, dating back thousands of years. A common thread through much of these traditions is a desire to gain something spiritual by giving up something physical.

Second, fasting has a distinct purpose! For centuries, people have understood that fasting helps detach us from the cravings and temptations of the world, to focus the mind and heart on deeper hungers and yearnings. For us today, it is a way to "make the complete gift of self to God."

Overall, fasting can force us to look more deeply into how we live and what we consume, and to think more intently about what really matters, which naturally turns our hearts and minds to our God. We give up far more than food. We give up control, power, the ability to have what we want when we want it, and present ourselves before God with complete humility, dependency, and trust.

Reflect

Fasting has ancient roots in many cultures and religious traditions. In a sense, because of that, fasting binds us together. How can I help myself feel connected to other peoples around the world through fasting?

If fasting is a "spiritual arm to do battle against disordered attachments," what are the attachments I'm seeking to fight?

A Prayer of Humility

Creator God, you who gave us the earth and all it contains know only too well what secrets reside in my heart, and where they are leading me. I come before you in a moment of complete surrender as I prepare to fast. I depend on you for life, for sustenance, for courage, for hope. I bow before you today to surrender all. I am yours. Help me to use this time to fully realize and profess my dependence on you, and to trust completely in your love. I will become less so that you may become more. Lead me to fulfill your will for my life. Amen.

2
How Fast Is Too Fast? Some Practical Pointers

My wife will be the first to tell you that I tend to jump into the pool without looking to see how deep the water is. This lack of caution can lead to errors in judgment, not just at the pool, but in life in general.

Many people jump too quickly when eager to start something new, and this includes the hard work of fasting. While the fundamental purpose of fasting may be spiritual, the actual practice of fasting has consequences that are undeniably physical. When you undertake a fast, you are undertaking an exercise that, even in small doses, can strain the spirit and tax the body. You should be prepared.

The good people at the Cleveland Clinic have compiled a short list of tips for fasting. You can find many other resources online or at your local library that may offer additional ideas that contain good old-fashioned common sense. In the Catholic tradition, St. Benedict, in his famous *Rule*, prescribed one meal a day for his monks, but also encouraged them to "love fasting." (Loving fasting may be more difficult for people nowadays to swallow, so to speak.) The saint wrote: "Renounce yourself in order to follow Christ (Mt 16:24; Lk 9:23); discipline your body (1 Cor 9:27); do not pamper yourself, but love fasting."

Well, I love chocolate. Do you think it's possible to have the same love for *doing without chocolate*?

I'm not convinced. But there is something key to this idea — moderation. Benedict again and again encouraged moderation. In his *Rule*'s prologue, the saint wrote that he wanted to offer "nothing harsh, nothing burdensome." He prescribed flexibility, adaptability, some measure of mercy. We need to be merciful toward others, yes, but also toward ourselves, in all areas of life, which includes our practice of fasting.

Being merciful toward ourselves brings me back to that advice from the Cleveland Clinic. If you want to undertake a meaningful fast that won't leave you physically spent, here are some tips.

1. Ease into it.

Start cutting back bit by bit over several days. You don't want to shock your body or wake up in the middle of the night screaming for just one more slice of pepperoni pizza. Your body is used to a certain amount of stimulation and a steady number of calories, and it won't take kindly to being deprived. Be gentle with your body and your spirit. If you slip into a fast gradually, the process will be easier and will more likely bring success.

How do you ease into a fast? Lower your sugar intake — cut out those cookies and soft drinks! — and fill up on carbs and protein.

You'll feel better, and fuller, and your family will probably find you're a lot less cranky, too!

2. Drink lots of water.

We hear a lot about staying hydrated. Your body needs water for everything to keep running smoothly — and you need it to keep up your strength.

3. Slow down.

As you ease into a fast, do not add additional stress to your body. You shouldn't start training for a marathon or add new exercises to your gym routine. Save your energy for things like getting the mail, doing the laundry, and praying. Especially praying. Fasting is a spiritual exercise, and you need those other muscles — in your mind, soul, and heart — to keep you going!

4. If you take medications, take care.

"Plan ahead" is how the Cleveland Clinic states it. First and foremost, talk to your doctor about what you will be doing and whether you need to adjust your medications. Some prescription drugs need to be taken with food; others need to be taken under certain circumstances to treat certain disorders (seizures or heart conditions). Be diligent, and be smart.

5. Just as you eased into a fast, you need to ease out of it, too.

You may be tempted to think: "Great! Now it's time for that cheesecake! And some ribs! And beer! I'm dying for a keg!" Not so fast, fasting person!

To put it simply: Don't end a fast with a feast. Be gentle with your body so it doesn't get overwhelmed by calorie overload (as tempting as that Big Mac might be). As you break your fast, spread your increased intake over a couple of meals, or a couple of days. Your blood sugar won't go nuts, and you won't find yourself craving a long nap at 10:00 a.m. You'll have more energy, feel better, and be able to focus your attention on looking back on your period of fasting, reflecting on what you gained from it and spending some time in a prayer of thanksgiving.

We do this, after all, to draw closer to God and to detach ourselves from the needs of this world. You might consider keeping a journal during your fast or taking a few minutes to record what you are experiencing, thinking, missing, and praying over. (I'll offer a thought or two about that later.)

Fasting shouldn't be easy, but it shouldn't be unbearable. We should approach fasting by looking not only at what we give up but also at what is given to us in return. We may lose a pound or two, but what do we gain? Clarity. Thoughtfulness. Empathy. All this and more!

Reflect

As we prepare to fast — whether for an hour or for a day — it's good to ask ourselves not only why we are undertaking a fast but also what we want to achieve from it. Bring this question to prayer: How can I improve my prayer life, my communion with God, during this time?

And then: How can I draw up a plan to make my fasting manageable and healthy — both spiritually and physically?

A Prayer for Patience

O Father of all plans, who told Jeremiah, "I know well the plans I have in mind for you," help me to plan my life according to your will, and to plan prayerfully and joyfully for my fasting. Help me to be patient when I am restless, to be careful when I am impulsive, to be hopeful when I am discouraged, to be gentle with myself when I feel most critical. Give me the grace to undertake this fast with a spirit of self-denial, purpose, and peace. Direct my efforts and bless me with the gift of discipline so that I may get the most from this time of sacrifice. Finally, Lord, I ask that you guide my thoughts and direct my yearnings away from this world and toward the next, where I pray I will be united with you forever. Amen.

3
Not So Fast: Hold On! Do I Really Have to Do This?

Right about now, you're probably asking yourself if this is necessary. Does the Church require me to do this? Is it optional?

Or to echo a phrase I heard a lot in high school: Will this be on the final?

Let's take a minute to look at what the Church has to say about fasting and its close cousin, abstinence. People often confuse the two, so let's make the distinction right here.

Abstinence means giving up certain foods during specific periods of time. During Lent, that means specifically giving up meat on Ash Wednesday and all the Fridays of the season.

Fasting, on the other hand, is abstaining from all food or, as one dictionary puts it, "to eat only sparingly."

Are there special times when we are supposed to do this? Glad you asked. The United States Conference of Catholic Bishops (USCCB) offers this helpful clarification on their website:

> Ash Wednesday and Good Friday are obligatory days of fasting and abstinence for Catholics. In addition, Fridays during Lent are obligatory days of abstinence.
>
> For members of the Latin Catholic Church, the norms on fasting are obligatory from age 18 until age 59. *When fasting, a person is permitted to eat one full meal, as well as two smaller meals that together are not equal to a full meal.* The norms concerning abstinence from meat are binding upon members of the Latin Catholic Church from age 14 onwards. (emphasis added)

The *Code of Canon Law* puts it this way:

> The divine law binds all the Christian faithful to do penance each in his or her own way. In order for all to be united among themselves by some common observance of penance, however, penitential days are prescribed on which the Christian faithful devote themselves in a special way to prayer, perform works of piety and charity, and deny themselves by fulfilling their own obligations more faithfully and especially by observing fast and abstinence, according to the norm of the following canons.
>
> The penitential days and times in the universal Church are every Friday of the whole year and the season of Lent. (Canons 1249–50)

You'll note that the Church requires some form of penance every Friday. Not so very long ago, in the days before the Second Vatican Council, that meant "meatless Fridays." I have vivid memories of opening my lunch bag every Friday when I was in grade school to enjoy a tuna sandwich or, if I was lucky, peanut butter and jelly. And in our popular culture, history shows that the genius who started serving fish sandwiches at McDonald's cornered the Catholic market on Fridays. Nowadays, we have the option of continuing to do that, or giving up something else as a sacrifice — maybe going without TV, or deciding to skip dessert or forgoing some other favorite food. The point is to invoke a personal penance — some small suffering for our sins or the sins of our broken world. Ultimately, as St. Thomas Aquinas put it, we fast "in order that the mind may arise more freely to the contemplation of heavenly things."

Now that we've covered what fasting truly is, we can return to the earlier question: Do we really have to do this?

Well, nowhere in the teachings of the

Catholic Church is fasting listed as "optional." In fact, the *Catechism of the Catholic Church* refers to fasting as one of "the precepts of the Church" (2041, 2043), something that is obligatory to help us grow in loving God and loving our neighbor.

Let's pull down from the shelf a copy of the *Catechism* and flip it open to paragraph 1434:

> The interior penance of the Christian can be expressed in many and various ways. Scripture and the Fathers insist above all on three forms, fasting, prayer, and almsgiving, which express conversion in relation to oneself, to God, and to others. Alongside the radical purification brought about by Baptism or martyrdom they cite as means of obtaining forgiveness of sins: efforts at reconciliation with one's neighbor, tears of repentance, *concern for the salvation of one's neigh-*

bor, the intercession of the saints, and the practice of charity "which covers a multitude of sins."

The *Catechism* goes on to say:

> The seasons and days of penance in the course of the liturgical year (Lent, each Friday in memory of the death of the Lord) are intense moments of the Church's penitential practice. These times are particularly appropriate for spiritual exercises, penitential liturgies, pilgrimages as signs of penance, voluntary self-denial such as fasting and almsgiving, and *fraternal sharing* (charitable and missionary works). (1438, emphasis added)

What we realize here is that a fast should take us far beyond ourselves. We're uniting our lives, our longings, and our sufferings with the sufferings of others around the world.

The *Catechism* explicitly talks about relationships with "our neighbor" and "fraternal sharing" that lead us more deeply to fulfilling Christ's second great commandment — to love our neighbor as we love ourselves.

Finally, there is one more period of fasting that the Church requires: the Eucharistic fast, which specifies not eating or drinking anything — except, if necessary, water and medication — for one hour before receiving holy Communion. For many years, until the 1950s, this fast began at midnight. Pope Pius XII shortened it to three hours. Pope Paul VI made it one hour.

In 1953, Pope Pius XII gave a beautiful explanation for the Eucharistic fast:

> Abstinence from food and drink is in accord with that supreme reverence we owe to the supreme majesty of Jesus Christ when we are going to receive him hidden under the veils of the Eucharist. More-over, when we receive his precious

Body and Blood before we take any food, we show clearly that this is the first and loftiest nourishment by which our soul is fed and holiness increased. (*Christus Dominus*)

Reflect

Fasting is a discipline that can connect us more closely to our suffering neighbors around the world. Who are some of those neighbors that you can pray for, pray with, pray about during a fast?

In many ways, fasting connects us with all those who hunger and thirst. However, not all hunger for food or thirst for water. What are some of the other things people hunger for in the world today?

A Prayer for Those Who Must Do Without

Father of mercies, guide me in my actions to do more than just give up something, but, in that sacrifice, to give. Teach me through fasting to give of myself — my thoughts, my prayers, my works, to unite my meager hardship with the sufferings of those around the world who hunger for food, for shelter, for dignity, for work; who yearn for respect, for friendship, for love. So many of my brothers and sisters around the world do without. May my sacrifice help me to feel closer to them, and draw me, also, closer to you. Amen.

4
Getting Started: It's Been an Hour; Give Me a Cookie!

Get ready, get set ... wait a minute. Are you ready?

What are your goals?

Maybe you will fast a full day. Maybe your fast will go longer. You begin with the noblest intentions.

Then after a short time, an hour or two, you might find yourself thinking: "Is it time to eat yet? Where are those Oreos?"

Um ... no. Let's rewind the tape and start over.

The best way to begin a fast and prevail through the inevitable pangs and rumblings is to set out with a trusted companion. I'm speaking, of course, of Jesus.

Find something holy to read — the Bible is always a good choice. Or maybe you would prefer a book about the saints, people who can teach us all a thing or two about rearranging priorities so we don't focus on the gallon of mint chocolate chip ice cream waiting in the kitchen freezer.

Fasting Pro Tip

Keep a bottle of water at hand. Water can help you feel full without, you know, *eating that ice cream*, and it can help us remember that fasting is, in part, about connecting with what is essential.

Now, find a quiet place to sit. Get comfortable. Take a deep breath. Make the Sign of the Cross.

And pray.

Prayer at the Beginning of a Fast

Heavenly Father, as I begin this time of fasting, this I pray: Lord, be my strength, my protector, my comfort, my food. Nourish me

with your peace. Refresh me with your love.
Enrich me with your grace. Jesus, you knew
hunger and loneliness during your days in
the desert. Help me to feel less alone during
this fast. Uplift me when I feel weak. Support
me when I feel tempted. Help me to keep my
eyes fixed on you and to see in your eyes the
suffering eyes of my brothers and sisters in
all their hunger and yearning. Holy Spirit, inspire me to find in my own yearnings
and cravings a deeper yearning for intimacy
with you. Reawaken in my heart your gifts:
wisdom and understanding, counsel and
fortitude, piety and knowledge, and fear of
the Lord. Direct my thoughts beyond my
own weakness — what I have done and what
I have failed to do — that I may emerge from
this fast renewed and restored. Amen.

Here at the outset, take just a few minutes
of quiet time to reflect on why you are undertaking this fast, and ask God to lead you
where he wants you to go.

If you want a humbling way to start, try

reading the Gospel account of the time Jesus spent in the desert in Matthew 4:1–11. We encounter this passage at the beginning of Lent, but it can be challenging and inspiring to rediscover it on our own time, as we undertake our own period of fasting with new eyes as we fast voluntarily.

After fifteen or twenty minutes, take a swig of water (or two or three), take a deep breath, and stretch your legs before heading out the door and getting on with your day.

Fasting shouldn't be relaxing or passive, but rather purposeful, even as you continue with your daily routine, living a normal life in every way possible (except without all those trips that take you out of your way to Dunkin' Donuts for an afternoon sugar fix).

In truth, the spirit of fasting is a spirit of cheerful self-denial, going about your day, but without, you know, eating.

That doesn't mean it's an exercise in public starvation or martyrdom. Jesus, after all, had this helpful tip for his apostles when they were fasting: "When you fast, anoint your head and wash your face, so that you may not appear to others to be fasting, except to your Father who is hidden. And your Father who sees what is hidden will repay you" (Mt 6:17–18). Dedicate this fast to "your Father who is hidden." You may be amazed at what happens.

Reflect

As his time in the desert came to an end, Jesus faced temptations. What are some of the temptations in your own life that you must confront? What are some of the needs you want fulfilled? Take some time during your fast to bring these to God in prayer and offer them to him as part of your sacrifice.

Find opportunities during your fast to pray to "your Father who is hidden," asking him to help direct your heart and strengthen your resolve. Turn to Jesus for consolation and support. He's been there — he knows what you are going through!

A Prayer in Time of Temptation

Compassionate Jesus, you faced difficulties and temptations during your fasting in the desert. Be with me as I face my own difficulties and temptations. Inflame my heart with love. Strengthen my will with courage. Be with me and help me face my hardships. Direct my thoughts, hopes, and desires to one purpose: to be united with you and to grow in grace. Amen.

5
The Hunger Games

Although you can fast from other luxuries, fasting from food is probably the most widely practiced form of fasting, and in the ancient tradition of the Church it is also the kind of sacrifice that can be the most arduous and physically taxing. Fasting is demanding. Anyone who's tried just a basic Lenten fast on Good Friday will tell you: Everything in the kitchen suddenly becomes irresistible when you can't even have a bite. Liver and onions? Yes, please! And don't scrimp on the onions! Say, is that broccoli in the refrigerator?

Still, the Catholic Church's rules on fasting aren't nearly as strict as they once were; we're never asked to fast for longer than a day and, even then, we're allowed one full meal. You could almost undergo a fast without even thinking about it. ("Gee, I was in meetings all day. Did I forget to eat lunch again?") However, the point of fasting is that it needs to be a conscious effort. For a fast to be fruitful, we *need* to think about it. The sacrifice needs to be intentional. A fast needs to have focus and purpose and make us at least a little bit uncomfortable. What's the point of a sacrifice if we don't realize something is missing?

Let me offer five quick pointers that can help give direction and focus — and, most importantly, purpose — to your fast. They might help you stay on track, particularly if you find yourself leaving the track to wander into the kitchen to see if the Oreos are missing you. (Trust me, they're fine.)

1. Make your fast a prayer.

As the hours tick by on a fasting day, it can help to pause for a moment every hour to whisper a brief prayer (an Our Father or Hail

Mary will do) and offer it for a particular intention. How often, when we were growing up, did we hear someone tell us, "Offer it up." Okay. *Offer it up.*

- Offer this hour for the hungry children of Ukraine, or Ethiopia, or Appalachia.
- Offer an hour for those who are addicted to drugs or alcohol for guidance to becoming clean.
- Offer part of your fast for people in broken homes or broken marriages who hunger for a sense of security and domestic peace.
- Offer your fast for extended family members, especially those you avoid or don't like, and for the healing of relationships.
- Offer your fast for your own weaknesses and failings. Pray

for God to help you improve.

- Offer up your growling stomach as your own hunger for holiness.

I'm sure you can think of many other worthy offerings. The important thing is to make your sacrifice matter.

2. Don't think so much about what you're missing, but about what you're gaining.

You're undertaking this exercise, in part, to draw closer to God and express solidarity with the sufferings of his Son and the many other people suffering in the world. Spend some time reflecting on what those forty days in the desert were like for Jesus and what he did to feel a closer connection to the particular human needs and yearnings of the human race. As he did that for you, what are you willing to do for him?

3. Take the time you would normally spend having lunch (or even dinner) and spend it with some holy reading.

As I mentioned earlier, keep a Bible nearby. Among other things, Bible readings will redirect your thoughts and serve as a (so to speak) little palate cleanser. Find a quiet place to just get away, turn down the noise of life, and focus on reading something besides that irresistible endless scroll of social media. Read the life of a saint or something written by a saint. Imagine the sacrifices that one holy soul made for God and his people. Imagine what his or her life must have been like. Imagine if you could come close to that! Our history is dotted with ordinary people who did extraordinary things. We stand on the shoulders of giants. Humble yourself and pray for inspiration and the guts to follow through with God's answer.

4. Got the time? Go to confession.

Fasting can help get your spiritual house in order, and celebrating the Sacrament of Reconciliation can do wonders to help that process. The grace of the sacrament can serve as a kind of booster shot during your time of fasting, helping you feel renewed and restored, like a spring cleaning of your body, mind, and soul all at once. You might consider confession as a fitting way to end a fast — maybe followed by a nice, healthy, moderate meal. (Remember: Don't end a fast with a feast!)

5. As the day winds on, never fail to give thanks. Often.

Giving thanks for the ability to fast is something easily overlooked, but we should never take it for granted. Having the opportunity and ability to fast means that you have been blessed: You have something to sacrifice. You are willing and able to do without, and to weather some small amount of hardship for a greater good. Thank God for that! Thank him for the gift of this moment, this opportunity, this chance to do something out of the ordinary. You have been blessed.

Reflect

Fasting can and should be a form of prayer.

- What do you want to say to God during this time?
- What intentions do you want to bring before him?
- What do you think he is trying to say to you?

Use this as an opportunity to listen. As St. Benedict put it, "Listen with the ear of the heart" to discern God's plan for your life.

When you feel pangs of hunger, ask yourself, "What am I truly hungering for?" Is it something more than food? Search your heart. Take a moral inventory. Take it to God in prayer and pray gratefully for every gift God has shared with you. Give thanks for the blessings you have! They may be more numerous than you realize.

A Prayer of Thanksgiving During a Fast

O God of abundance, during this time of fasting, of giving up, I can never thank you enough for all that I have been given. Your gifts enrich me, inspire me, console me, and feed me in the midst of my deepest hungers. When I hunger for love, you are there. When I hunger for peace, you are there. When I hunger for hope, you are there, bringing light into my darkest hours. At this time of sacrifice, I pray for those who also feel hunger of all kinds, and pray that they may know your limitless love and feel your comforting embrace. I ask this, through the One who remains your greatest gift to our broken world, your Son, Jesus Christ. Amen.

6
Food for Thought: Fasting from Other Temptations

When most of us think of fasting, we think of food. (I mentioned a rumbling stomach earlier. How's that going?) But in this day and age, there can be other things that we crave just as much — maybe more. Giving them up can be a great exercise and, very often, a challenging sacrifice.

Most of these things are unhealthy for us anyway, to one extent or another. Fasting from them can help remove some of the clutter and noise from our lives and bring us more closely to the ideal we all strive for — the imitation of Christ.

Where should you begin? Here are some

ideas. I'm sure you can think of others.

Fast from Social Media

Many people give up Facebook, Instagram, and every other social media platform for Lent. Some brave souls limit the time they devote to answering emails or sending texts; they may do it for an hour in the morning and an hour in the evening.

I'll admit, as someone who spent most of my life working in media, this is tough. I mean, *really tough*. When I've tried to detach from my cell phone, I still find myself instinctively reaching for it while waiting in line or riding the subway. I go through withdrawal and experience real pangs of social media hunger. But the benefits of doing without social media cannot be overstated. Fasting from Facebook or chat rooms means fasting from snark, chatter, pettiness, cruelty, conspiracy theories, and ad hominem attacks, and stepping away from the rock-throwing trolls who thrive on negativity. The social media world can be brutal. It's healthier to see life from a gentler, more constructive perspective.

Fast from Television

Do people still watch TV? I think so. (I know I do!) Not so very long ago (when I was growing up), the sisters who taught us would recommend giving up TV for Lent. (That was unthinkable, of course. Who could live without watching cartoons on Saturday morning? And give up *Batman*? Never.) But in the era of the twenty-four-hour news cycle, when we subsist on a steady diet of talking heads, when cable and streaming services pump endless programming into our homes — telling us how to cook, what to eat, how to decorate, and what to think — we all can use a break. Fasting from television can help us think more clearly and, believe it or not, the break may lead you to rediscovering the dying art of conversation.

Fast from Gossip

Pope Francis likes to talk about this a lot, and

I think he may be on to something.

Once upon a time, our tribal forebears gathered around the water cooler to swap small talk at the office — and a lot of that talk was very small. Even petty. It was gossip. If the water cooler wasn't available, there was the corporate cafeteria. And there was always the telephone after hours.

Our human nature leads us to whisper and spread speculation about others and, in our worst moments, to take smug satisfaction in their problems. While the Gospels offer many accounts of Jesus sharing in our humanity, there is no evidence he ever gossiped. That should tell us something.

Pope Francis put it bluntly a few years ago during a general audience at the Vatican. "Gossip is not a work of the Holy Spirit; it is not a work of the unity of the Church," he said. "Gossip destroys the work of God. Please stop gossiping."

Fasting from gossip enables us to focus our minds and hearts on our own salvation — instead of busying ourselves with the lives and problems of others. It can keep our attention where it belongs, reminding us of what really matters.

Fast from Despair

I know, despair can't just be shut off like a faucet. Some days, troubles weigh us down and relationships burden us. Whether we want to or not, we just feel miserable. If you find yourself easily drawn to thoughts that are skeptical, cynical, critical, or just plain gloomy, use your time fasting to concentrate on eradicating those feelings. Make a resolution that for just one hour or one day you will draw back the curtains and let in the light. Stop negative thoughts before they start.

Be as purposeful in directing your attitude as you are with your fasting.

Trust in God's mercy and providence. Believe in hope. As Jesus prepared to return to his heavenly Father, he said, "Do not let your hearts be troubled" (Jn 14:1).

Have faith that the God who created our world will not abandon it — or you!

A good way to fast from despair is to feast on gratitude. "Give thanks to the Lord for he is good" (Ps 118:1).

Reflect

What are some of the modern pleasures you enjoy that you don't want to give up? How would your perspective change without them in your life?

We're all familiar with the proverb "count your blessings." What are the blessings in your life?

Prayer for Fasting in the Twenty-first Century

Father of all creation, help me to fast from the temptations of modern life: the noise, chatter, gossip, and superficial distractions that so often turn my heart away from you. Help me instead to walk a path toward holiness. Grant me the courage to be quiet, the humility to be giving, the compassion to be understanding, the desire to be more like Jesus. In a world grown cynical and of-

ten cruel, I pray that you give me the grace,
hour by hour, day by day, to look away from
what is hurtful, to focus on what is hopeful.
Be with me in my efforts to atone for what I
have done and what I have failed to do, and
help me become all you dream for me to be.
Amen.

7
Fast Friends: Fasting as a Group

Fasting is generally considered a solitary, private activity — something between you, God, and the cookie jar. But can it be a communal event? Can you fast as a group?

While this isn't widespread in the Catholic Church, several Christian denominations have promoted so-called corporate fasting — which is not fasting from corporations (as attractive as that might sound) but fasting as a body of people in a small organization or group. To borrow a phrase from *High School Musical*, it's holding on to the idea that "we're all in this together."

Certainly, the early Christians did that. Let's look at this reference from the Acts of the Apostles: "While they were worshiping the Lord and fasting, the holy Spirit said, 'Set apart for me Barnabas and Saul for the work to which I have called them.' Then, completing their fasting and prayer, they laid hands on them and sent them off" (13:2–3).

Just as praying and worshiping as a group has immeasurable benefits, there are a lot of blessings to be had by fasting collectively. It builds a support system; it helps you feel like you aren't doing it alone; and it gives a sense of shared purpose. There is strength in numbers!

So how to begin?

1. Identify a cause.

There is no shortage of causes or intentions worth fasting over. Maybe you'd like to fast for an end to war, to promote pro-life action in your local legislature, or to unite in prayer to support your pastor or bishop, or even the pope. Determine how you want to focus your energies. Then get to it!

2. Form a group of like-minded people.

If you want to do this as a parish, reach out to your pastor and get his support (or, even, his participation). There may be small groups within the parish that would be eager to join this effort — a social action group, an outreach ministry, or a prayer circle.

3. Determine the specifics of your fast.

Something modest — a one-day fast, or even half a day — is manageable and, for many people, doable. Figure out where and when you want to undertake this. You might start with a Liturgy of the Word at the parish, followed by reflections offered by members of the group, and maybe some music. Conclude this part by breaking bread (literally) to give you some nourishment as you begin your fast. You might add a praying of the Rosary, or even praying the Way of the Cross. You might consider promoting the event on social media and even posting live updates or encouragement during the fast. The possibilities are endless.

4. Form a prayer circle for the fast.

After you go your separate ways, call one another for support, inspiration, prayers, and pep talks. You could get together for a bread-and-water meal midway through the fast or to pray another Rosary. Again, this could be a great opportunity to celebrate the Sacrament of Reconciliation.

5. Conclude your fast with another liturgy — and a modest meal!

A suitable conclusion could be celebrating Mass together, or perhaps a Holy Hour with Adoration and Benediction. You could ask participants to share reflections and prayers focused on the intention of the fast. Afterward, gather for a simple meal — either at the church hall or a local restaurant. Take time to talk about the experience, share insights and challenges, and reflect on what you gained from the fast. If you're ambitious, you might even set a date for the next one!

Make this an event that is **manageable, shareable,** and **doable.** The group can be as large or as small as you wish — though a more modest head count will give it a sense of intimacy and family.

Most importantly, keep prayer at the center of this activity. Keep it God-focused. Ultimately, you want to do this to support an intention and to move hearts — beginning with your own.

Reflect

A fast can be a powerful and unifying force in a local community. What causes or concerns would a group of people want to pray about in a corporate fast?

Prayer for a Group Fast

Almighty God, as we begin this fast together, we come to you in humility and trust, asking you to bless our efforts and guide our sacrifice. Accompany us on our journey and keep us ever mindful of your abiding love and mercy. Strengthen our resolve, enflame our hearts, uplift our purpose, and send your Spirit to renew us in mind and body, so that we can make of this time a sacrificial offering that can help make of our world a place of justice, compassion, and peace. We ask this through your Son and our brother, Jesus Christ. Amen.

8
One Last Bite: Some Final Thoughts

After a good meal at a favorite restaurant, you usually feel contentedly stuffed and perhaps look forward to a long nap — or maybe look at your calendar to see when you can go back for a second helping.

Think you'll feel that way after a fast?

Fat chance.

As you find your way to the freezer and become reacquainted with the Oreo cookie ice cream that's been patiently waiting for you, you might discover you actually feel unexpectedly full.

Full of a very different kind of satisfaction — and peace.

Full of gratitude.

Full of, well, *grace.*

Don't be surprised if you feel blessed.

If you've been able to approach the act of fasting as a prayer — as a gift to God, as an offering of humility and hope, as an expression of quiet penance and solidarity and sacrificial love — you may end up looking at yourself and the world differently. You may come to a deeper appreciation of all you have, of all that that God has given you, and of what it feels like to just give up a little of that for a brief moment in time.

While you're searching for the chocolate sauce to go with the ice cream, try a little soul-searching, too.

How has this experience changed you?

Are you at a different place than you were when the fast began? (I don't just mean sitting at the kitchen table.) Where has this journey taken you?

Try this:

- Summarize how the fast made

you feel in just six words. (Avoid the easy ones: "hungry," "cranky," "testy.")

- Maybe complete this sentence: "Fasting made me …

- Write a short letter to God, perhaps a thank you note to the Creator, or a simple prayer of resolution and hope, or a message of contrition, refocusing your energies in the days going forward.

The fast may be over. But something else is beginning.

Hear that?

No, it's not your stomach rumbling. It's the Holy Spirit. He'd like a word with you. Take some time. Listen. You might be surprised at what you hear.

Prayer of Thanksgiving after a Fast

Generous God, thank you for the gift of this fast — the gift of giving up something I can have, to experience for a short time what it is to want, and to realize, in all my wanting, my greatest desire is you. Thank you for an opportunity to pray, to search my heart, to reflect more deeply on all that I am, and all that you want me to be. Thank you for this blessed chance to grow, to reflect, to share in some small way in the sufferings of others, so that I can understand more fully the sufferings and sacrifices of your Son. With your grace to guide me, help me to attain what I truly crave: the deepest union with you that satisfies every hunger, now and forever. Amen.

About the Author

Deacon Greg Kandra is an author, speaker, blogger, and award-winning journalist who is perhaps best known as the creator of the popular blog *The Deacon's Bench* (thedeaconsbench.com). He was ordained a deacon for the Diocese of Brooklyn in 2007. Deacon Greg and his wife live outside Orlando, Florida.

You might also like:

The Handy Little Guide to Novenas

By Allison Gingras

The Blessed Mother and the Twelve Apostles remained in the Upper Room in prayer for nine days after the Lord's ascension. From those nine days of prayer, the tradition of novenas — praying for a specific period of time for a special intention — was born. The word *novena* is derived from the Latin *novem*, meaning nine.

In this brief booklet, author and novena enthusiast Allison Gingras helps you understand and practice this ancient, yet totally relevant, form of prayer.

Available at
OSVCatholicBookstore.com
or wherever books are sold

You might also like:

The Handy Little Guide to Prayer

By Barb Szyszkiewicz

God knows what's on our minds and in our hearts, but we still need to verbalize our innermost thoughts, feelings, and intentions. That's prayer.

In this easy-to-read, down-to-earth introduction to conversation with God, you'll discover, or rediscover, what you need to be able to "pray without ceasing." Author, mom, wife, and Secular Franciscan Barb Szyszkiewicz helps you strengthen your connection to God through prayer.

You might also like:

The Handy Little Guide to Confession

By Michelle Jones Schroeder

Confession. Reconciliation. Penance.

It's a sacrament with many names, but most of us seem to have a similar reaction to it: Do I have to go? It's been too long. Doesn't God already know I'm sorry? I don't remember how to do it. I'm embarrassed. I'm scared.

Michelle Schroeder has been there. She admits to skipping Reconciliation for years… until she realized that, to experience God's mercy most fully, she needed to ask for it.

You might also like:

The Handy Little Guide to Adoration

By Michelle Jones Schroeder

You will not only explore the nuts and bolts of Eucharistic Adoration but also discover great reasons and times to enter into the presence of Jesus in the Eucharist, including when:

- Life is moving fast and you need to be refreshed
- You need answers and direction from a loving God
- You need focus in prayer
- You're experiencing spiritual dryness
- You need to prepare for the Sacrament of Reconciliation.